SOUL ON FIRE

The True Story of John O'Leary's Survival After a Devastating
Fire and His Journey to Find Hope and Purpose

Soren Valliard

Copyright

© 2025 Soren Valliard. All Rights Reserved.

This book, including its content, images, graphics, and other materials, is protected by copyright law. All rights to the contents of this book are reserved. No part of this book may be reproduced, stored in a retrieval system, or transmitted in any form or by any means electronic, mechanical, photocopy, recording, or otherwise without the prior written permission of the copyright holder, except for brief quotations used in reviews or for educational purposes in accordance with applicable copyright law.

Disclaimer

The opinions and interpretations expressed in this book are solely those of the author(s) and do not reflect the views of the filmmakers, production companies, or any individuals associated with the films discussed. The information provided in this movie review guidebook is for general informational and entertainment purposes only.

While every effort has been made to ensure the accuracy of the information in this book, the author(s) cannot guarantee that all content is fully accurate, complete, or up-to-date. Film releases, availability, and other details (such as cast, crew, and plot summaries) are subject to change over time and may vary by region or platform.

All trademarks, service marks, and trade names used in this book are the property of their respective owners, and their use does not imply any affiliation, endorsement, or sponsorship by the respective owners.

The author(s) of this guidebook do not assume any liability for the accuracy, completeness, or reliability of the information presented. Readers are encouraged to verify information independently and to check for updates regarding movie releases, content availability, and film-related details through official sources such as the film studios and streaming platforms.

By using this book, you agree to accept full responsibility for any actions taken based on the information provided.

TABLE OF CONTENT

Chapter 1: A Story of Survival – The Movie's Foundation 13
    The True Story of John O'Leary 13
    From Tragedy to Triumph: How the Movie Captures John's Life 15
    Themes of Resilience, Hope, and Family 18
    The Director's Vision: Sean McNamara's Approach to Telling the Story 19

Chapter 2: The Cinematic Experience – Analyzing the Film 21
    Opening Scene Breakdown: Setting the Stage for John's Story 21
    Key Moments: A Step-by-Step Analysis of the Most Pivotal Scenes 23
        The First Surgery: A Moment of Despair 24
        The Introduction of Jack Buck: A Source of Light in the Darkness 25
        The Moment of Reflection: Coming to Terms with the Scars 26
    Cinematography and Visual Storytelling: Capturing Emotion Through Film 27
    The Role of Music and Soundtrack in Enhancing the Narrative 29

Chapter 3: The Emotional Impact – How the Movie Resonates 31
    The Power of John O'Leary's Journey on the Big

Screen..31
Viewer Reactions: The Emotional Pull of the Story 33
How the Film Makes Audiences Reflect on Their
Own Lives...35

Chapter 4: Characters and Performances................ 39
Joel Courtney as John O'Leary: A Perfect Portrayal
of Resilience.. 39
William H. Macy as Jack Buck: The Symbol of
Mentorship and Hope... 41
Supporting Cast: How They Contribute to the Story's
Emotional Depth..43
The Chemistry Between Characters and Its Impact
on the Film's Success... 45

**Chapter 5: The Real John O'Leary – A Young Boy
Who Defied All Odds..48**
John O'Leary's Life Before the Fire: A Snapshot of
His Childhood..48
The Devastating Accident: How a Simple Mistake
Led to Tragedy...50
The Road to Recovery: How John's Body and Mind
Healed..52
The Influence of Faith, Family, and the Community
in John's Recovery...55

Chapter 6: The Legacy of John O'Leary's Story..... 57
From Survivor to Speaker: How John Inspires People
Worldwide..57
The Release of On Fire and the Beginning of the
Movement..60
Why John's Story Continues to Touch Lives Across

Generations..62

Chapter 7: Bringing the True Story to Life: A Behind-the-Scenes Look..65

The Challenges of Adapting a Real-Life Story for the Screen.. 65

How the Filmmakers Stayed True to John O'Leary's Story...68

Interviews with the Director and Cast on Creating the Movie.. 70

Filming in St. Louis: The Significance of Location 72

Chapter 8: The Screenplay – Crafting the Story from Real Events..74

Adapting John O'Leary's Memoir into a Film Script.. 74

Balancing Accuracy with Cinematic Creativity...... 77

Key Dialogues and Monologues That Define the Film...80

Chapter 9: Filmmaking Techniques: Visualizing Hope and Struggle...82

Using Color and Lighting to Portray Emotion........ 82

Special Effects and Realism in the Depiction of the Fire...85

The Power of Flashbacks: Telling John's Story Within a Story..88

Chapter 10: Overcoming Adversity – Lessons from John's Journey...91

The Importance of Resilience in the Face of Tragedy. 91

How the Movie Inspires Viewers to Never Give Up...

93

    Finding Strength in Vulnerability: Embracing Pain to Heal..96

Chapter 11: Faith and Hope – Core Themes in Soul on Fire..99

    The Role of Faith in John O'Leary's Recovery....... 99

    Hope as a Central Theme: The Motivation Behind the Film.. 102

    Spirituality and its Representation in the Movie... 104

Chapter 12: Conclusion – A Story of Hope, Strength, and Unbreakable Spirit..107

    Wrapping Up the Story Behind Soul on Fire......... 108

    Final Thoughts on the Impact of John O'Leary's Journey..109

    What Audiences Can Take Away from the Film... 111

Introduction: The Significance of Soul on Fire

Soul on Fire stands as a remarkable testament to the resilience of the human spirit, telling the true and extraordinary story of John O'Leary, a young boy who defied impossible odds after a horrific accident. Directed by Sean McNamara, the film takes us through an emotional rollercoaster, recounting how John went from being a victim of a life-altering tragedy to an inspirational speaker whose story touches the lives of millions. The film is not just about surviving physical trauma, but about the mental and emotional transformation that happens when one chooses hope, faith, and resilience in the face of overwhelming adversity.

The film's impact resonates deeply because it emphasizes a universal truth, our capacity to persevere even when all seems lost. *Soul on Fire* is not just a movie about a young boy's fight for survival; it is a reflection of the transformative power of hope and community. It touches on themes of family, faith, mentorship, and healing. More than that, it provides a window into the heart of what it means to rebuild after tragedy, to rise again and be reborn stronger than before.

John O'Leary's journey is one of profound change and growth. While the film captures the intense moments of his recovery, it also highlights the transformative role played by those around him, particularly his family and the renowned sports announcer Jack Buck, whose support helped John through some of his darkest moments. Their bond is central to the narrative, demonstrating the powerful effects of human connection and encouragement.

The significance of *Soul on Fire* extends beyond its narrative. It is a reminder of the potential for growth even in the aftermath of trauma. For viewers, it is a film that invites them to reflect on their own lives, to consider how they might face their struggles, and to find strength in unexpected places.

A Brief Overview of John O'Leary's Journey

John O'Leary's journey from suffering to self-empowerment is one of the most powerful real-life stories you could imagine. When he was nine years old, a tragic accident forever altered his life. Playing in his garage, John inadvertently caused a devastating fire, one that left him with burns covering more than 80% of his body. The severity of his injuries led to a long and painful recovery, both physically and emotionally. For most, such an experience would be insurmountable, but John's story is one of remarkable survival, not only overcoming his physical challenges but transforming them into an opportunity for healing and growth.

The road to recovery was neither quick nor easy. John underwent extensive surgeries and endured years of physical therapy. The sheer agony of his medical treatments was only rivaled by the emotional toll. The scars on his body were reminders of the trauma, but they became, over time, symbols of his inner strength. His parents played an irreplaceable role in his healing process, offering unwavering support and love through every stage. His mother's words of encouragement and his father's stoic presence gave him the emotional fortitude to push through when it seemed like there was no way forward.

But it wasn't just his family that helped him navigate this arduous journey. His story was also shaped by those who came into his life, particularly the legendary sportscaster Jack Buck. Jack, who had his own history of overcoming challenges, became a mentor to John, offering a lifeline in moments when the young boy felt hopeless. Jack's friendship was pivotal, providing not only encouragement but a sense of direction. John's relationship with Jack was one of the most significant in his life, and it became a foundational element of John's recovery.

John eventually became a powerful motivational speaker, using his voice to inspire others to face their own obstacles and to never give up, no matter how difficult life may seem. His story, encapsulated in his bestselling book *On Fire: The Seven Choices to Ignite a Radically Inspired Life*, has reached millions of people around the world. It's a message of hope, resilience, and the human spirit's capacity to rise after being broken.

The film *Soul on Fire* serves as a visual and emotional journey that brings to life John's incredible story. Through the actors' performances and the skillful direction, viewers are taken through the harrowing moments of John's accident and the subsequent years of recovery. The film does more than tell the story of a survivor; it paints a vivid picture of a young boy's transition into adulthood, learning to not only live with his scars but to embrace them as a source of power and purpose.

Purpose of This Book: A Movie Review and Behind-the-Scenes Insight

The purpose of this book is to provide an in-depth review and analysis of *Soul on Fire*, while also offering a unique perspective on the film's deeper meaning. This book will explore how the film captures the essence of

John O'Leary's life, offering an emotional recounting of his struggle and recovery. By delving into the film's narrative, cinematography, performances, and underlying messages, this book aims to offer readers a comprehensive understanding of what makes *Soul on Fire* a truly inspiring cinematic experience.

In addition to the review, the book will also take a look behind the scenes, exploring the making of the film, the challenges of adapting such a powerful true story, and the creative choices that brought John O'Leary's journey to life on the big screen. From casting decisions to the portrayal of key moments in John's life, we will examine how the filmmakers achieved their vision and stayed true to the heart of the story.

Through a detailed analysis of key scenes, character development, and filmmaking techniques, this book will give readers a deeper appreciation for the art of storytelling. It will also provide insights into how movies based on real-life events can serve as vehicles for healing, growth, and inspiration.

This book is for anyone who has seen *Soul on Fire* and wants to understand the layers of meaning woven throughout the film. It is also for those who may not have seen the movie yet but are interested in the profound journey of John O'Leary and the lessons his life story holds. Whether you are a fan of biographical films or someone who seeks motivation from true stories of triumph, this book will offer a fresh and detailed perspective on a film that has touched so many.

By exploring the significance of *Soul on Fire* in a broader context, we can appreciate not only the artistry behind the film but also the power of storytelling to inspire change. John O'Leary's story is one that transcends the screen, it is a living, breathing testament to the power of the human spirit. Through this review, we aim to honor that spirit and share the lessons it has taught us all.

Chapter 1: A Story of Survival – The Movie's Foundation

The True Story of John O'Leary

John O'Leary's story is nothing short of extraordinary. It is the kind of story that both challenges and inspires, one that invites us to reflect on what it means to truly survive, to grow, and to transcend the hardships that life often throws our way. At the age of nine, John was faced with an unimaginable ordeal that would leave scars, both physical and emotional, for the rest of his life.

The tragedy began on an ordinary day in 1987, when John and his friends were playing in the family garage in St. Louis, Missouri. As they were playing with fire, something went horribly wrong. A nearby can of gasoline exploded, igniting a fire that would consume John's body and change the course of his life forever. His injuries were severe, over 80% of his body was burned, and the doctors who first treated him gave him little chance of survival.

The accident didn't just affect John physically; it was a trauma that reached deep into his soul. As he lay in a hospital bed for months, undergoing more surgeries than most people would ever encounter in a lifetime, the young boy was forced to grapple not only with the pain of his wounds but also with the overwhelming sense of fear and hopelessness that comes with such a devastating event. There were times when John was told that he wouldn't make it, that his life would be forever marked by the physical and emotional scars of the fire. Yet, despite the overwhelming odds stacked against him, he defied them.

The road to recovery for John was long, grueling, and full of setbacks. Yet, it was also marked by moments of profound grace, strength, and courage. John's family was there by his side every step of the way, providing him with unwavering support and love. His mother, particularly, was a source of constant encouragement, telling him that he was more than his scars and that the journey ahead, though difficult, would eventually lead to a brighter future.

Through his recovery, John discovered the power of hope and faith. It wasn't just the medical staff or his family that helped him survive, it was his internal will to fight. His sense of purpose became rooted in the idea that his life had meaning beyond the physical. The accident could have easily consumed him, but instead,

John found a new direction. He chose to become a beacon of hope for others who faced their own struggles, realizing that the scars he carried were not just reminders of trauma, but symbols of his ability to overcome adversity.

John's story is more than just a survival tale; it is one of transformation. From tragedy, he built a life dedicated to inspiring others. He became a motivational speaker, using his story to ignite hope in those who felt broken or defeated. His journey from victim to victor is encapsulated in his book *On Fire*, where he lays out the lessons he learned throughout his extraordinary life.

From Tragedy to Triumph: How the Movie Captures John's Life

When *Soul on Fire* was brought to the screen, the challenge was to translate the immense depth of John's life into a visual and emotional experience that would resonate with viewers. Sean McNamara, the director, faced the task of adapting John's incredibly personal and painful journey into a narrative that would engage and move audiences while staying true to the core of John's story. The film's creators knew that in order to do justice to the significance of John's life, they would need to portray not only his pain and suffering but also the profound strength he exhibited in rising above it.

The movie begins by depicting the innocence of John's childhood, capturing his joy and youthful energy before the accident. Through careful attention to detail, the film paints a picture of a typical boy, a child full of life, laughter, and hope. But that hope is soon shattered by the horrific explosion that leaves John fighting for his life. In these early scenes, the film doesn't shy away from the rawness of the tragedy. The images are haunting, the intensity palpable. It pulls no punches in showing the physical horror of the burns, the uncertainty of John's future, and the terror that gripped his family.

From this tragedy, however, the movie seamlessly transitions into John's journey of recovery. The pacing of the film slows as it takes viewers into the grueling world of hospital rooms, endless surgeries, and the emotional strain that John's family had to endure. These scenes are poignant, yet there's always an underlying sense of hope, as the movie focuses on John's inner strength and the support of those who loved him. One of the most powerful aspects of the film is how it captures John's internal struggle, not just the battle for his life, but the emotional and mental toll that healing took.

The film also places a strong emphasis on the relationships that helped John heal. One of the most significant relationships in John's recovery was his bond with Jack Buck, a beloved sports announcer in St. Louis. Buck became a mentor to John during his hospital stay, offering words of encouragement and hope when the boy felt completely lost. This relationship is captured beautifully in the film, as it becomes a symbol of the power of mentorship and the importance of human connection in times of crisis. William H. Macy plays Jack Buck with a quiet strength, embodying the character's warmth and steadfast belief in John's potential.

The transition from tragedy to triumph is executed with remarkable precision in the film. As John begins to heal physically, he also starts to reclaim his sense of self-worth. The emotional depth of his recovery is portrayed through his interactions with family, friends, and medical staff, as well as his internal monologue, which speaks to the struggles he faces while learning to embrace his scars. This emotional journey is brought to life by Joel Courtney, who plays John with such raw vulnerability and strength that it's impossible not to be moved by his performance.

Themes of Resilience, Hope, and Family

At the heart of *Soul on Fire* is the theme of resilience. John O'Leary's journey is a testament to the unbreakable strength of the human spirit, and the movie beautifully illustrates how resilience isn't just about enduring; it's about overcoming and growing stronger through adversity. The film shows us that resilience isn't something that can be learned overnight, it is forged through experience, often born from pain and suffering.

The story of John's recovery is a vivid reminder that resilience is not just a personal trait but one that can be nurtured by those around you. Family plays a crucial role in John's journey, and the film highlights how the O'Leary family's unwavering love and support were essential to his survival. It wasn't just John who fought for his life; it was his family who fought alongside him, standing by his side through every surgery, every setback, and every triumph. The family dynamic is beautifully portrayed, with the nurturing strength of John's mother and the quiet, determined presence of his father creating a foundation of love that allowed him to rebuild his life.

Hope is another central theme in the film. As John's story unfolds, we see how hope becomes a lifeline, first through the medical staff who believed in his recovery, then through the friendships and connections he made along the way. John's relationship with Jack Buck is emblematic of how hope can be nurtured through human connection. Buck, played by William H. Macy, is not only a mentor but a symbol of the kind of hope that allows us to push through our darkest moments. Buck's belief in John, even when John couldn't believe in himself, serves as a powerful reminder of how crucial it is to have someone who believes in you when you're at your lowest.

The movie also underscores the importance of community and connection. It shows how John's healing was not just a solitary journey, it was one shared with the people who loved him, as well as the strangers who helped him along the way. The presence of a strong community provides the emotional scaffolding that supports John's recovery. This theme resonates deeply, reminding viewers of the importance of leaning on others and offering support when someone is struggling.

The Director's Vision: Sean McNamara's Approach to Telling the Story

Sean McNamara's direction of *Soul on Fire* is nothing short of masterful. Known for his ability to handle emotionally complex stories, McNamara brings a sensitive, nuanced touch to the film. His direction captures the raw intensity of John's story while also highlighting the moments of hope, triumph, and human connection that defined John's journey.

McNamara's vision for the film was clear from the start: he wanted to make sure that the story wasn't just about a boy who survived a horrific accident but about the transformation that followed. The story of survival was just the beginning, what made John's life so remarkable was the way in which he used his pain as fuel to inspire others. McNamara understood that the heart of the story lay in the emotional and spiritual journey that John went on, not just the physical recovery.

To achieve this, McNamara employed a combination of realistic, visceral moments and quieter, more intimate scenes that allowed the characters' emotions to take center stage. By alternating between intense, physical moments of pain and quieter, reflective moments of healing, McNamara creates a balance that mirrors John's own experience. The visual elements of the film, particularly the way in which John's emotional recovery is portrayed, are both poignant and powerful, offering the audience a glimpse into John's internal world.

Chapter 2: The Cinematic Experience – Analyzing the Film

Opening Scene Breakdown: Setting the Stage for John's Story

The opening scene of *Soul on Fire* is one of the most crucial moments in the film, not only because it sets the emotional tone for the rest of the movie, but because it introduces the audience to the life-altering event that will define the entire narrative. This is the moment when viewers are first confronted with John O'Leary's tragic accident. It's raw, it's immediate, and it draws us in from the very first frame.

The scene begins innocuously enough, with a typical summer afternoon in St. Louis. John, played by Joel Courtney, is shown playing with friends in the garage. There's a lightness in the air, a sense of youthful adventure and innocence. The camera lingers on John's face as he smiles, a typical kid enjoying the summer heat. The color palette used here is warm, golden, almost nostalgic. It's clear that this is a moment of carefree happiness.

Then, in a split second, everything changes.

The camera cuts to a close-up of the can of gasoline, which, after a moment of hesitation, ignites. The explosion that follows is chaotic and terrifying. The film's pacing shifts dramatically from calm to intense, mirroring the suddenness of the accident. The soundtrack grows tense, heightening the tension. The visceral reaction is immediate; you can feel the heat and the destruction as the flames engulf the scene. The rapid editing and sharp cuts between John's face, the fire, and the chaos around him disorient the viewer, placing them directly into the panic-stricken moment.

As the fire rages, we see John's desperate attempts to escape, but the world around him is collapsing. The sound design here is brilliant. The crackling of the fire is deafening, and every scream, every breath, feels amplified. It's clear that this moment is more than just the physical trauma of the fire, it's the emotional trauma that will follow. There's no gentle build-up, no warning. The explosion shatters the viewer's expectations, setting the stage for a story of resilience, survival, and hope.

What makes this opening scene so powerful is the way it balances the horror of the fire with the subtle emotional undertones. While the fire itself is the immediate threat, there's a quiet tragedy in John's realization of what's happening. His childhood, his innocence, is being ripped away in a moment of youthful carelessness. As the flames rise, so too does the awareness of the magnitude of the disaster.

Through this opening, the film's tone is firmly established. This is not just a story of physical survival. It's a story of transformation, of rebirth, of a life that's about to change in ways unimaginable. The intense, heart-pounding opening pulls us into John's world, showing us the beginning of his journey into a life that would forever be marked by fire.

Key Moments: A Step-by-Step Analysis of the Most Pivotal Scenes

As the film unfolds, it is punctuated by a series of pivotal moments, each one contributing to John's emotional and physical journey. These scenes are not merely markers of plot progression; they are deeply emotional turning points that shape John's character and narrative. Here, we'll explore some of the most significant moments in *Soul on Fire*.

The First Surgery: A Moment of Despair

One of the earliest moments in the film that truly encapsulates John's emotional and physical struggle is his first surgery. After being rushed to the hospital, John is immediately placed in intensive care, where his burns are assessed, and the magnitude of his injuries becomes apparent. The scene is emotionally harrowing, as we witness John's confusion, fear, and pain as doctors and nurses work around him.

The decision to show this moment in such an unflinching way allows the audience to understand the gravity of the situation. John is not just fighting for survival; he's fighting against the kind of trauma that could break a person. As the medical team preps him for surgery, Joel Courtney's performance captures the vulnerability of a child in the face of something so incomprehensible. His fear is palpable, and it draws the audience into his emotional state. There is no dramatization of the pain; instead, it's portrayed as a quiet but intense ordeal that speaks to the rawness of his struggle.

This pivotal moment is also important because it marks the beginning of John's transformation. His body may be broken, but the audience begins to see the faint glimmers of the willpower that will carry him through. This scene lays the groundwork for his eventual emotional and mental strength. The struggle is internal as much as it is external, and it's something we'll see evolve throughout the rest of the film.

The Introduction of Jack Buck: A Source of Light in the Darkness

One of the film's most emotionally significant moments is when John meets Jack Buck, the iconic sportscaster, who becomes a pivotal figure in his recovery. Played by William H. Macy, Buck's character is portrayed as calm, steady, and unwavering, offering John a sense of stability and hope in a time when everything around him feels chaotic.

In a moment that exemplifies the power of mentorship, Jack enters John's life at a critical juncture. After John has been through a series of surgeries and is facing the reality of his new life, Jack offers him words of encouragement. He doesn't sugarcoat the situation; instead, he tells John that life isn't fair and that things won't be easy. But what Jack offers isn't false hope, it's a challenge. He tells John that if he wants to truly live, he has to choose to live. This moment of wisdom becomes a defining point for John, and for the audience, it is one of the most heartwarming moments of the film.

Macy's portrayal of Jack Buck is pitch-perfect. His steady presence contrasts sharply with the chaos of John's physical and emotional state, offering the audience a much-needed respite from the intensity of the earlier scenes. Jack Buck's belief in John is something that, at this point in the story, John doesn't yet believe in himself. Yet, through this relationship, John begins to see that his life has value beyond his scars.

The Moment of Reflection: Coming to Terms with the Scars

A key turning point in John's recovery is when he finally faces the full extent of his scars. For much of the film, John is shown in various stages of recovery, both physically and emotionally. But it's not until later in the movie that we see him fully confront the reality of his appearance. This is a pivotal moment in the film because it marks the point where John must choose to accept the new version of himself.

This scene is portrayed with a quiet intensity. John, standing in front of a mirror, takes in his reflection for the first time. The camera lingers on his face as he looks at the scars, processing the magnitude of his transformation. There is no music here, no dialogue, just the quiet sound of his breathing. This raw moment speaks volumes about the internal struggle he is facing. It's a moment of reconciliation, where John begins to accept that his scars are not signs of weakness, but symbols of survival. It's one of the most poignant moments in the film, and Joel Courtney's performance is subtle yet powerful in conveying the emotional weight of this scene.

The silence in this scene speaks to the internal conversation that John is having with himself. There's no dialogue because none is necessary. The reflection in the mirror speaks louder than any words ever could. Through this moment, John's true transformation begins. He stops seeing himself as a victim of tragedy and begins to embrace himself as a survivor.

Cinematography and Visual Storytelling: Capturing Emotion Through Film

The cinematography in *Soul on Fire* plays a crucial role in conveying the emotional depth of John's story. From the very first scenes, the film uses lighting, framing, and color to underscore the emotional undertones of the narrative. Each shot is carefully constructed to reflect the tone and atmosphere of the story being told. The decision to use warm, golden hues during the scenes of John's childhood adds a layer of nostalgia and innocence, while the cooler, more muted colors used in the hospital scenes reflect the stark reality of his pain and suffering.

One of the most effective visual storytelling techniques in the film is the use of contrast. In the scenes of John's recovery, the camera often isolates him, showing him alone in a hospital bed, surrounded by sterile white walls. This stark contrast serves to emphasize the emotional isolation that John feels. At times, the camera lingers on his face, capturing the subtle shifts in his expression as he processes the overwhelming circumstances surrounding him. These close-ups allow the audience to feel what John is feeling, to understand his loneliness, his fear, and his determination.

As John begins to heal, the cinematography shifts. There is a gradual transition from the stark, sterile environment to more natural, warmer tones. The scenes set in the family home, for instance, are shot with a sense of intimacy and warmth, symbolizing the healing that takes place within the framework of love and support. This shift in color and lighting represents John's emotional recovery and his ability to rebuild his life.

The visual choices in *Soul on Fire* are not just aesthetic; they are integral to the storytelling. Every frame reflects the emotional journey that John is going through, whether it's the desolation of the fire, the isolation of his recovery, or the warmth of his eventual rebirth.

The Role of Music and Soundtrack in Enhancing the Narrative

Music plays a pivotal role in amplifying the emotional impact of *Soul on Fire*. The film's soundtrack, composed by Mark Isham, serves as an emotional undercurrent, heightening the film's most intimate and powerful moments. From the opening sequence to the final scenes, the music works in harmony with the visuals, enhancing the emotional depth of John's journey.

In particular, the music during the more somber moments, such as the surgery scenes and the moments of John's internal reflection, adds another layer of emotional resonance. The subtle, delicate piano melodies, paired with the sparse orchestration, reflect the vulnerability and fragility of John's emotional state. The score is never overpowering, but rather it gently supports the narrative, allowing the audience to fully immerse themselves in John's emotional experience.

During scenes of hope and triumph, the music shifts to a more uplifting and inspiring tone. The crescendo of the score mirrors John's internal transformation, underscoring the idea that, despite the pain and suffering, there is always the potential for growth, for renewal, and for finding light in the darkest of circumstances.

Chapter 3: The Emotional Impact – How the Movie Resonates

The Power of John O'Leary's Journey on the Big Screen

There are few stories that have the power to deeply stir the soul the way John O'Leary's journey does. The film *Soul on Fire* doesn't just recount the story of a young boy who survived an unspeakable tragedy; it pulls the audience into the very heart of his transformation, making us feel the intensity of his pain and the radiance of his eventual triumph. What makes John's story so powerful, and what makes the film adaptation so emotionally resonant, is the profound sense of humanity at the core of it.

From the very first moments of the film, John's ordeal is presented in such a raw and visceral way that the audience cannot help but be pulled into his experience. The accident is not a distant event; it is immediate, real, and devastating. We feel the heat of the flames as if we're right there with John, caught in the explosive moment of terror. The pain, both physical and emotional, is palpable in every scene that follows.

The journey to recovery is painstakingly slow, each step forward marked by struggles with immense physical, mental, and emotional pain. But what *Soul on Fire* does masterfully is to show the transformation that happens beyond the surface. Yes, John's body is scarred, and yes, his recovery is long, but the real power of his journey lies in how he learns to embrace his scars, not as something to hide or to mourn, but as part of who he is, a symbol of survival, strength, and ultimately, rebirth.

Joel Courtney, who portrays John, brings this story to life with exceptional depth and sensitivity. He doesn't just play a boy who survived a tragic accident; he plays someone whose life has been forever altered by that experience, someone who is struggling to reconcile the new version of himself with the boy he once was. His performance is subtle but powerful, capturing the complexity of John's emotional world. From the moments of anger and despair to those of hope and courage, Courtney's portrayal of John resonates with anyone who has faced adversity and struggled to find a way forward.

In bringing this story to the screen, the filmmakers succeed in making John's journey feel universal. It's not just about one boy's survival; it's about the human capacity to endure, to grow, and to ultimately find meaning in even the darkest moments. The film doesn't just portray his physical recovery, it dives deep into the emotional and psychological transformation that follows a traumatic event, making us reflect on our own capacity to heal and grow after life's challenges.

Viewer Reactions: The Emotional Pull of the Story

It's rare for a film to leave a lasting emotional impact long after the credits roll, but *Soul on Fire* achieves this with remarkable success. The movie's ability to evoke raw, genuine emotions in its audience is one of the reasons it has resonated with so many. From the moment the audience is introduced to John, there's an immediate connection, one that deepens as the story unfolds. What makes this film so powerful is that it taps into something universal, the human experience of suffering, survival, and ultimately, hope.

When the film first premiered, audience reactions were overwhelmingly positive. Viewers were moved not only by the heart-wrenching depiction of John's accident and recovery but also by the way the film emphasized the strength of the human spirit. Many expressed how they were unable to hold back tears during certain scenes, especially during the most emotional moments, such as John's first encounter with Jack Buck, the moment he faces his scars in the mirror, and his eventual realization that his journey wasn't just about survival, but about embracing life in all of its complexities.

There is a vulnerability in the film that strikes a chord with everyone who has ever faced hardship or loss.

When John confronts the harsh reality of his new appearance, when he struggles with self-acceptance, and when he falters and then finds strength in the love and support of his family, the audience is reminded of their own personal struggles, their own moments of self-doubt, and their own paths to healing.

Perhaps the most powerful aspect of the film is how it invites the viewer to reflect on their own lives. John's journey is not just his own; it is a mirror for our own trials and triumphs. As the film explores themes of resilience, family, and finding hope in the midst of suffering, it prompts audiences to reflect on their own sources of strength. It challenges them to reconsider how they approach adversity and whether they too have the inner strength to rise above their own challenges.

The emotional pull of the film lies in its ability to connect on such a personal level. It doesn't rely on grandiose speeches or over-the-top dramatizations; instead, it presents John's story in a quiet, raw, and authentic way that allows the audience to experience his journey as if it were their own. Whether it's through a shared moment of grief, the universal desire for acceptance, or the deep yearning for hope, *Soul on Fire* speaks to something deep inside all of us.

How the Film Makes Audiences Reflect on Their Own Lives

What sets *Soul on Fire* apart from other films that deal with themes of trauma and recovery is its ability to inspire self-reflection. While the film is undeniably John O'Leary's story, it has a universal appeal because it addresses questions of identity, survival, and resilience that transcend individual experience. The film doesn't just ask the audience to look at John's struggle; it challenges them to look at their own lives and reflect on how they handle adversity.

For many viewers, *Soul on Fire* serves as a catalyst for introspection. It asks: How would I respond in John's shoes? Would I have the strength to endure such pain and emerge with a sense of purpose and hope? Would I be able to find meaning in my scars, both literal and metaphorical?

John's transformation is one of the most compelling aspects of the film. He begins as a frightened, vulnerable boy and gradually evolves into a resilient, hopeful young man. His journey challenges us to think about our own personal growth and how we cope with life's challenges. We all face obstacles, whether they are physical, emotional, or psychological, and the film prompts us to consider how we handle those moments. Do we allow ourselves to be defined by our suffering, or do we rise above it, transforming our pain into something that empowers us?

The film also challenges the viewer to think about the role of community and support in overcoming difficulties. John's healing process is deeply intertwined with the love and support of his family, the mentorship of Jack Buck, and the connections he forms with those around him. This theme highlights the importance of not facing adversity alone and serves as a reminder that we all need people to help us through our darkest times. For many, the film prompts reflection on the relationships in their own lives and how they can offer support to others who are struggling.

In addition, *Soul on Fire* makes viewers question how they see others who are struggling. The way John faces the world with his scars and learns to embrace them instead of hiding them forces us to confront our own biases and assumptions about physical appearance, strength, and vulnerability. How often do we judge others based on their external circumstances, without recognizing the internal battles they may be fighting? The film challenges us to approach others with more empathy, compassion, and understanding.

Perhaps one of the most profound aspects of the film is its ability to inspire hope. John's journey isn't just about overcoming obstacles, it's about transforming the very meaning of those obstacles. By the end of the film, viewers are left with a renewed sense of purpose. The message is clear: no matter how difficult life may seem, there is always the possibility for healing, growth, and redemption. For many, the film is a powerful reminder that even in the most dire of circumstances, there is always hope.

Conclusion: How the Film Resonates with Audiences

In many ways, *Soul on Fire* is not just a film; it's a mirror that reflects back to the viewer their own struggles, strengths, and desires for growth. Through John O'Leary's powerful journey, the film resonates deeply, encouraging audiences to reflect on their own lives and how they approach challenges, both large and small. It's a story that transcends John's personal experience and speaks to the universal human condition, making it not only a compelling tale of survival but also a testament to the power of the human spirit.

The emotional impact of *Soul on Fire* is undeniable. It leaves audiences with a renewed sense of hope, a deeper understanding of resilience, and an appreciation for the relationships that shape us. More than just a biographical film, it is an invitation to look inward, to recognize our own capacity for transformation, and to embrace the power of hope in the face of adversity.

Chapter 4: Characters and Performances

Joel Courtney as John O'Leary: A Perfect Portrayal of Resilience

In *Soul on Fire*, the role of John O'Leary is undeniably one of the most complex and emotionally demanding portrayals of resilience and transformation. Joel Courtney, known for his ability to bring emotional depth to his roles, delivers a performance that is nothing short of extraordinary. From the very beginning of the film, Courtney embodies John's innocence, vulnerability, and ultimate strength, crafting a character that is simultaneously relatable and inspiring.

Courtney's portrayal of John captures the sheer humanity of the young boy who finds himself thrust into a situation beyond his control. The film opens with John's joyful, carefree childhood, a boy full of life and hope. Through Courtney's nuanced performance, we see John's innocence before the tragedy strikes, and then we are quickly thrust into the horrors of the fire. This stark contrast between joy and terror, played so effectively by Courtney, makes the trauma that John experiences feel even more real.

As the story progresses, Courtney skillfully navigates John's transition from a frightened and deeply wounded child to a young man who learns to embrace both his scars and the lessons learned through his pain. The emotional range required for this character is immense. Courtney moves seamlessly from moments of anguish and despair to those of quiet reflection and eventual acceptance. In particular, the scene in which John first faces his reflection in the mirror is a standout moment of self-realization. The vulnerability and internal struggle he displays are powerful; Courtney's subtle expressions convey a deep sense of turmoil as John grapples with the physical and emotional changes he must now face.

One of the most poignant aspects of Courtney's performance is how he conveys John's internal battle between feeling like a victim of circumstance and finding empowerment in his survival. The physical pain John endures is palpable, but it's the emotional complexity of his journey that Courtney brings to life with precision. Through every small gesture, every change in his posture, and every word spoken, he channels the character's evolving sense of hope and self-worth. It's a performance that quietly demands respect, as it carries with it not only the weight of John's journey but also the profound resilience that defines it.

Courtney doesn't simply play a victim; he plays a survivor, someone who has learned to find strength not in spite of his suffering, but because of it. His performance serves as the emotional backbone of the film, making John's story resonate with anyone who has ever faced hardship or struggled to find hope.

William H. Macy as Jack Buck: The Symbol of Mentorship and Hope

The role of Jack Buck, the iconic sports announcer and mentor to John O'Leary, is brought to life by the legendary William H. Macy. As Jack Buck, Macy provides a comforting and steady presence in the film, offering not only a source of wisdom but also an anchor for John during his darkest moments. Macy's performance is a masterclass in understated yet impactful acting.

Jack Buck's character could have easily fallen into the archetype of the wise mentor, offering platitudes and general guidance. However, Macy transforms this role into something far more nuanced. He doesn't present Buck as some idealized figure of invulnerability. Instead, Buck is portrayed as a man who has faced his own share of struggles and loss, someone who understands the weight of suffering, but who also believes in the power of perseverance.

Macy's performance excels in its quiet strength. One of the most powerful moments between Buck and John occurs when Jack first visits John in the hospital. The scene could have been one of overt melodrama, but Macy infuses it with a sense of calm and authenticity. There is no need for excessive speeches or dramatic declarations. Instead, Jack Buck offers John something more profound: a belief that he can survive and even thrive, despite the odds. Macy's quiet but forceful delivery conveys a sense of understanding that cuts through the fog of John's despair.

In Buck's relationship with John, Macy showcases the power of mentorship. He doesn't offer easy answers; rather, he gives John something much more valuable: the belief that he is capable of finding his own way forward. The chemistry between Macy and Courtney is palpable, Buck's faith in John is unwavering, and his quiet confidence becomes the foundation upon which John builds his own sense of purpose. Macy's Jack Buck is not just a mentor; he is a guiding light in the storm of John's recovery.

Macy's portrayal of Buck brings depth to the character. It is not just about guiding John through physical recovery, but about showing him how to reclaim his life in a world that has been irreversibly changed. Through his performance, Macy demonstrates that mentorship is not always about giving someone the answers, it's about encouraging them to find their own strength, and Buck does this with compassion, patience, and an unshakeable belief in John's potential.

Supporting Cast: How They Contribute to the Story's Emotional Depth

While Joel Courtney and William H. Macy are undoubtedly central to the narrative, the supporting cast in *Soul on Fire* plays a crucial role in enriching the emotional layers of the story. Each actor, no matter the size of their role, brings something invaluable to the film, creating a world around John O'Leary that feels both authentic and deeply human.

One of the standout performances in the supporting cast comes from John's mother, played by **Stéphanie Szostak**. Her portrayal of a mother who is watching her child endure unimaginable pain is both heartbreaking and beautiful. Szostak conveys a mother's fierce love and determination, as well as her moments of fear and doubt. There are several moments in the film where Szostak's character is called upon to show not just concern for John's recovery, but a kind of emotional fatigue. She is strong for her child, but her own suffering is clear in every line and gesture. This adds a layer of depth to the film, making it not just about John's recovery but about the toll that trauma takes on those around him.

John's father, played by **John Corbett**, offers a quiet but powerful presence. His role may not be as overtly dramatic as some of the others, but his stoic strength serves as a counterpoint to his wife's emotional rawness and John's outward vulnerability. Corbett's performance is subtle yet profound. As the father of a child going through unimaginable pain, his character is often seen in the background, offering a steady hand and a calm voice. His character reminds us that strength doesn't always have to be loud, it can also be found in quiet endurance and the unwavering support of those we love.

Another key supporting role is that of **Masey McLain**, who plays one of John's caregivers during his recovery. While the role may not be as central as others, McLain's performance adds an essential layer of realism to the film's depiction of medical recovery. Her character's compassion and dedication to John's healing process highlight the incredible role that healthcare professionals play in helping people heal, not just physically but emotionally as well. McLain's chemistry with Courtney adds warmth and humanity to the hospital scenes, showing that even in the sterile environment of a hospital, human connection can still make a profound difference.

The supporting characters collectively contribute to the emotional depth of the film, making John's journey feel not just personal, but communal. Each actor, from John's family to the medical professionals who aid him, adds complexity to the film's portrayal of recovery and growth. Through these performances, we see that John's journey is not just about him, it's about everyone who plays a role in helping him rise again.

The Chemistry Between Characters and Its Impact on the Film's Success

One of the most important aspects of *Soul on Fire* is the chemistry between its characters. The relationships, particularly between John and those closest to him, form the emotional heart of the film. The connection between John and Jack Buck, played by Macy, is perhaps the most significant. Their dynamic is more than just that of a mentor and mentee, it is one of genuine care, mutual respect, and shared understanding.

Courtney and Macy's chemistry is palpable, as they effortlessly create a bond that feels natural and heartfelt. The way that Jack Buck believes in John's potential, even when John struggles to believe in himself, is beautifully conveyed through the performances of both actors. It's a relationship that feels earned, one that grows naturally over the course of the film. This connection allows the audience to invest in John's journey, knowing that Jack's guidance is more than just words, it's a deep, abiding belief in the power of hope.

Similarly, the bond between John and his family members, particularly his mother and father, is a cornerstone of the film. The performances from Szostak and Corbett help ground the film in reality, offering a portrait of a family that is united by love and resilience. The way John interacts with his parents adds authenticity to the narrative, showing that while John's journey is deeply personal, it is also a collective effort.

The chemistry between the cast members contributes to the film's success in conveying its emotional depth. The relationships feel lived-in, not forced, and the connections between the characters form the emotional backbone of the story. Through these bonds, the film explores themes of love, loss, and recovery, inviting the audience to reflect on their own relationships and the impact they have on one another's lives.

In *Soul on Fire*, the characters and their performances are key to making the film not just a retelling of John O'Leary's life, but a deeply emotional experience. Joel Courtney's portrayal of John brings the character's resilience to life in a way that resonates with audiences on a personal level. William H. Macy's Jack Buck serves as a beacon of hope and mentorship, reminding us of the power of human connection. The supporting cast, with their nuanced performances, adds layers of emotional depth, highlighting the importance of love and support in times of hardship. The chemistry between the characters makes the story feel real and impactful, allowing the film to shine as a powerful narrative of survival and triumph.

Chapter 5: The Real John O'Leary – A Young Boy Who Defied All Odds

John O'Leary's Life Before the Fire: A Snapshot of His Childhood

Before the tragic accident that would forever alter the course of his life, John O'Leary was a typical, energetic nine-year-old boy growing up in St. Louis, Missouri. Like many children of his age, John found joy in the simple pleasures of life, playing outside, riding his bike, and enjoying the companionship of friends and family. He had a mischievous side, a playful spirit that made him well-liked by his peers. The world, in his young mind, was full of possibility. He was the kind of child who radiated enthusiasm for life, quick to laugh and even quicker to engage in adventures that pushed the limits of his imagination.

John was close to his family, particularly his mother and father, who encouraged him to explore the world around him while maintaining a deep sense of responsibility and care. His parents, who are portrayed in the film by **Stéphanie Szostak** and **John Corbett**, were devoted to their children, creating a loving and nurturing environment in which John felt both safe and encouraged to pursue his dreams. The O'Leary family's home was a place of warmth and connection, and John's relationship with his siblings was filled with the playful camaraderie that defines childhood. He was the kind of boy who felt the love of his family deeply, even in the moments of quiet reflection.

In the film, the early scenes do an excellent job of showcasing John's joyful, carefree existence. There's an innocence in these moments that feels almost too perfect, as if the world was going to pause forever at this stage of his life. John had a clear sense of who he was before the fire, he was the adventurous, spirited boy who was filled with curiosity about the world. There is a certain sweetness in these moments, a simplicity that makes the tragedy to come all the more difficult to bear.

John's childhood was marked by a strong sense of optimism. He was a boy who had dreams, aspirations, and an innate belief that life was full of wonder. The film perfectly captures this spirit of youthful exuberance. This snapshot of John's life shows a young boy who wasn't yet aware of the fragility of life. He didn't know how quickly things could change. It's this innocence, this sense of invincibility that many children experience before they come face-to-face with the harsh realities of life, that makes the events that follow even more heartbreaking.

The O'Leary home was one filled with love and understanding, where John felt both seen and supported in everything he did. There's a recurring theme in the film, one that can be seen in John's relationship with his parents, that no matter how much time would pass or how much pain John would endure, he would always carry that love with him. His childhood, full of laughter and affection, laid the foundation for the strength that he would later draw upon in his darkest days.

The Devastating Accident: How a Simple Mistake Led to Tragedy

The accident that forever altered John O'Leary's life occurred on an ordinary afternoon, a day that started like any other. John, along with his friends, was spending time in the garage, a place where boys like him would often gather to play and experiment. It was a typical, carefree moment until one fateful decision set into motion a chain of events that no one could have predicted. What started as a harmless activity, playing with fire, turned into an unimaginable disaster.

The film does an incredible job of capturing the suddenness and intensity of the moment. In the blink of an eye, a simple mistake, knocking over a can of gasoline, turned into a fireball that would engulf John's entire world. The explosion that followed was violent, swift, and terrifying. The speed with which everything changed is depicted with breathtaking precision in the film. The sense of shock and terror is palpable. One moment, John is laughing and playing with his friends; the next, he is trapped in the blazing inferno, his body rapidly succumbing to the flames.

As the fire consumes the garage and John is overwhelmed by the smoke and heat, the film shifts from a lighthearted childhood moment to a horrific, gut-wrenching scene. The immediate aftermath is horrifying; John is left lying on the floor, barely conscious, with his skin burnt beyond recognition. His world, his childhood, is suddenly lost in a sea of pain and uncertainty. There's a stark contrast between the joyful boy we saw moments earlier and the mangled, suffering child now lying on the ground.

The film doesn't shy away from showing the brutality of the accident. The trauma is shown in its full, horrifying intensity. The special effects team worked tirelessly to create a realistic portrayal of the injuries John sustained, from the intense burn marks to the raw, painful reality of his condition. The decision to not sugarcoat the physical devastation John endured makes the tragedy all the more real and heartbreaking.

But what the film also does so effectively is show the emotional devastation. It's not just about John's injuries; it's about the terror his family felt when they were suddenly thrust into a nightmare they never imagined. His mother, portrayed with remarkable sensitivity by Szostak, is shown in a state of disbelief and horror as she sees her son, who moments ago was a lively and healthy child, now unrecognizable and fighting for his life. The emotional toll on John's family, particularly his parents, is just as intense as the physical injuries John sustained. It's a powerful reminder that trauma affects not just the person enduring it, but everyone around them.

The accident serves as a turning point, not just in John's life, but in the entire O'Leary family's journey. The film doesn't just focus on the moment of the explosion; it shows the ripple effect it has, how one single event alters the course of so many lives. In this way, the film underscores the fragility of life and the unpredictability of fate. In an instant, everything changed.

The Road to Recovery: How John's Body and Mind Healed

The road to recovery for John O'Leary was long, painful, and fraught with both physical and emotional challenges. The film carefully chronicles the many stages of his healing process, illustrating the immense difficulties he faced, not only in the physical healing of his body but also in the profound emotional journey of recovery. What stands out most in John's journey is the sheer willpower he summoned to push through the seemingly insurmountable obstacles.

In the hospital, John was subjected to numerous surgeries, each one aimed at saving his life and restoring some semblance of normalcy. The physical pain he endured was beyond anything most of us could imagine. The burn injuries left him with permanent scars, and the intense skin grafts that followed were not just physically taxing but emotionally draining. There were moments of despair when John questioned whether it was worth it, whether he could go on. The movie doesn't shy away from depicting these moments of vulnerability, showing John's internal battle as he grappled with the emotional scars that accompanied his physical ones.

Joel Courtney's portrayal of John's journey through recovery is raw and emotional. His performance captures the confusion and pain that John must have felt during his time in the hospital. The scene where John first tries to walk again, with his body weakened and his self-esteem at an all-time low, is a particularly powerful moment. There's no exaggeration here, just the quiet desperation of a boy who doesn't want to be a burden but who is weighed down by the gravity of his circumstances. Courtney's vulnerability in these scenes makes John's emotional recovery just as compelling as his physical healing.

John's healing wasn't just physical; it was a mental and emotional process. In the film, this aspect of recovery is represented by the deep inner strength that John gradually finds within himself. The quiet moments of reflection, where John contemplates his own identity and the future, are contrasted with the more external struggles of learning to walk, speak, and live again. The gradual rebuilding of John's identity is portrayed with remarkable sensitivity. It's not just about his body healing, it's about him reconciling the boy he was with the person he was becoming.

The film also highlights the crucial role of his family and the broader community in his recovery. John didn't go through this journey alone. His parents, siblings, and friends were there every step of the way. There's a powerful scene in which John's mother tells him that he is not defined by his scars, a sentiment that helps John reframe his self-worth. His family was instrumental in reminding him that his value didn't come from his appearance, but from who he was as a person. Through their unwavering love and support, John was able to rediscover his sense of self and find hope for the future.

The Influence of Faith, Family, and the Community in John's Recovery

One of the most profound aspects of John O'Leary's recovery was the role of faith, family, and community. These three pillars provided John with the foundation of support that he needed to heal both physically and emotionally. In the film, we see that it's not just John who struggles with the aftermath of the accident, his family, too, is on their own journey of healing.

John's faith, both spiritual and personal, was a major influence in his recovery. His belief in something greater than himself gave him the strength to endure the most difficult moments. The film touches on the importance of faith in John's journey, showing how it allowed him to find meaning in his suffering. It wasn't just about surviving; it was about finding a purpose through the pain. This sense of purpose was vital in helping John push through his darkest moments.

Family was equally central to John's recovery. His parents' love and steadfast belief in his ability to heal were constant sources of strength. His mother's unwavering support and his father's quiet strength allowed John to see the love surrounding him. These themes of love and faith were captured beautifully in the film, reminding viewers that healing isn't just a personal journey, it's one that's shared with others.

Finally, the broader community played a significant role in John's recovery. While the film focuses primarily on his immediate family, it subtly shows how John's journey resonated with others. The love and support he received from his doctors, his caregivers, and the local community in St. Louis helped to create an environment where healing could take place. It's a reminder that sometimes, the strength we need to recover comes from the people around us, whether it's the kind words of a stranger or the steady presence of loved ones.

Chapter 6: The Legacy of John O'Leary's Story

From Survivor to Speaker: How John Inspires People Worldwide

John O'Leary's transformation from a young boy who survived a devastating fire to a renowned motivational speaker is one of the most powerful aspects of his journey. After the traumatic accident, John could have easily retreated from the world, succumbing to the despair that often follows such a life-altering event. Instead, he chose a different path, one that would eventually lead him to inspire millions of people around the world.

The moment John's story began to take on a public life was when he realized that his pain, his survival, and ultimately his recovery had the potential to offer hope to others facing their own challenges. It wasn't simply about surviving the fire; it was about using the lessons learned from that experience to help others overcome their own obstacles. This realization would drive John to become a speaker, one who could use his voice to empower people to rise above their struggles, no matter how impossible they may seem.

The film *Soul on Fire* doesn't just focus on the aftermath of the fire, it also emphasizes John's decision to take control of his narrative. As portrayed by **Joel Courtney**, John's decision to become a motivational speaker didn't happen overnight. It was a slow realization, one that unfolded as he began to understand the profound impact his story could have on others. Throughout his recovery, John's family, particularly his mother, encouraged him to share his story, but it wasn't until he began speaking to others that John truly recognized the power of his experience.

John's story resonated with audiences from all walks of life, and the message was clear: no matter the circumstances, there is always the possibility of overcoming adversity. His path to becoming a speaker was not only an act of healing for himself but also an act of generosity. In sharing his pain and his triumphs, John gave people the courage to face their own challenges with renewed strength.

In the film, as John begins to speak publicly, **Courtney's portrayal** of his internal struggle is poignantly authentic. The audience watches as John steps out of his comfort zone, away from the protective cocoon of his family, and into the wider world. The vulnerability is raw, but so is the determination. In his first speeches, he faces doubts and fears, but the more he speaks, the more he realizes the tremendous impact his words have. This is one of the key emotional moments in the film, John starts out uncertain, but as he finds his voice, he begins to understand that his survival wasn't just a personal victory; it was something that could help others find their own courage.

The film depicts the moment when John first gets up in front of a crowd, sharing his story with people who are strangers to him, but who are, in many ways, also facing their own personal battles. The courage required to open up about such a traumatic experience is something that can't be understated, and **Joel Courtney** captures this vulnerability with great depth. In those early speeches, John's humility and raw honesty shine through, making his eventual success as a speaker even more inspiring.

As John began speaking professionally, he made appearances at schools, hospitals, and conferences, delivering motivational speeches that touched hearts and ignited hope. His message was simple, yet profound: no matter how bad things get, we all have the strength to rise above our circumstances. By sharing his own journey, John was able to provide people with the tools to overcome their own struggles, whether they were physical, emotional, or mental.

John's transition from survivor to speaker also highlights the importance of resilience. His own journey, from the depths of despair to finding purpose in his pain, was a powerful demonstration that survival isn't just about making it through tough times, it's about using those experiences to fuel growth and change. This idea became the core of his speaking engagements, as he sought to inspire others to not just endure hardship, but to use it as a stepping stone toward a better life.

As the film shows, John's growth into a speaker was closely tied to his healing process. He wasn't just telling his story; he was actively participating in his recovery, finding strength in the very act of sharing his experience with others. Through these speeches, he not only helped others but also began to solidify his own understanding of the impact his survival could have on the world.

The Release of *On Fire* and the Beginning of the Movement

In addition to his work as a speaker, John's story became even more widely recognized when he published his memoir *On Fire: The 7 Choices to Ignite a Radically Inspired Life*. The book was a natural extension of his speaking career, providing a deeper, more personal exploration of his journey, as well as the lessons he learned along the way. Through *On Fire*, John was able to articulate not just the details of his recovery but the deeper principles of resilience, hope, and personal growth that he had discovered through his experience.

The release of *On Fire* marked the beginning of a larger movement. The book was an invitation for people everywhere to reframe their understanding of pain and suffering. Through its pages, John challenged readers to not just survive their hardships, but to rise above them and transform them into opportunities for personal growth. The seven choices outlined in the book, such as embracing change, letting go of fear, and finding purpose in the pain, became a blueprint for people seeking to overcome adversity in their own lives.

The film *Soul on Fire* highlights the importance of this book, not only as a record of John's personal journey but as a guide for anyone facing struggles. John's story wasn't just about surviving; it was about thriving in the face of overwhelming odds. His book became a tool for empowerment, and through it, his influence expanded far beyond the confines of the stages he spoke on.

In the film, we see John sharing the message of his book with a broader audience, slowly building a following of individuals who felt inspired by his story and wanted to apply his lessons to their own lives. The process of writing *On Fire* was cathartic for John; it allowed him to take the lessons he had learned from his trauma and turn them into something tangible that could help others. It wasn't just about the narrative of survival, it was about turning that survival into a life-changing philosophy.

The book's impact is not confined to a specific group of people. While it resonated with those who had endured physical trauma, *On Fire* also connected with individuals facing emotional and psychological challenges. John's words spoke to anyone who had ever felt lost, afraid, or hopeless, offering them a roadmap for finding their way back to a place of strength and purpose.

The success of *On Fire* allowed John to expand his reach as a motivational speaker and leader. The principles in his book became part of a broader cultural movement that emphasized the importance of resilience, community, and personal empowerment. As the book became a bestseller, John's story began to touch even more lives, inspiring people across generations, cultures, and walks of life. The film captures the transformative power of John's journey, not just for himself, but for the thousands of people who found hope in his words.

Why John's Story Continues to Touch Lives Across Generations

John O'Leary's story continues to resonate because it taps into something timeless, the universal human experience of overcoming adversity. From the moment the fire changed his life, John became a symbol of resilience, but his message is not confined to any single moment in time. It transcends generations because it speaks to something inherent in all of us: the desire to live a meaningful life, to face hardships with courage, and to emerge stronger.

In the film *Soul on Fire*, John's transformation from victim to victor is presented as both a personal journey and a universal one. His story is a testament to the power of the human spirit to heal, grow, and inspire. Whether it's a child facing bullying, an adult grappling with personal loss, or someone struggling with a physical or mental illness, John's journey reminds us all that it is possible to rise above our circumstances. His story has a timeless quality, one that speaks to the challenges and triumphs that define the human experience.

As the film shows, John's influence reaches people of all ages. Whether he's speaking to a classroom of young students, a group of corporate leaders, or a community of individuals recovering from personal trauma, his words have the power to ignite something in others. The principles he shares, the importance of resilience, the need for connection, and the ability to find hope in the darkest moments, are universal truths that resonate across time and space.

John's message continues to inspire across generations because it is based on timeless values. His story reminds us that no matter how difficult life may get, we all have the potential to rise, to heal, and to find purpose. The film beautifully captures this idea, showing that John's legacy is not just in the stories he shares, but in the lives he touches and the changes he inspires.

The influence of John's story has spread far beyond the pages of his book and the stages where he spoke. It's a movement that continues to grow, fueled by the belief that anyone, no matter their circumstances, can rise above their challenges and create a life of meaning and purpose. John O'Leary's legacy is not just in the survival of a boy who defied the odds, it's in the lives he has changed and continues to change with his message of hope and resilience.

Chapter 7: Bringing the True Story to Life: A Behind-the-Scenes Look

The Challenges of Adapting a Real-Life Story for the Screen

Adapting a real-life story for the screen presents both profound challenges and unique opportunities. When it comes to a story as personal and emotional as John O'Leary's, the pressure to remain true to the essence of the journey while also creating a cinematic experience that resonates with audiences is immense. The filmmakers knew that they weren't simply telling the story of a boy who survived a tragic accident, they were capturing the story of an individual whose survival and transformation inspired millions around the world.

One of the primary challenges in adapting *Soul on Fire* was striking the right balance between staying faithful to John's life and creating a narrative that would engage a broader audience. John's life is rich with detail, filled with moments of both profound tragedy and remarkable triumph. The filmmakers needed to condense his life into a two-hour film without losing the essence of his emotional and psychological transformation. In particular, the complexity of John's recovery, both physical and mental, required careful handling to ensure that the film conveyed not just the medical details of his journey, but also the deeper emotional layers of what it meant to heal, to rebuild one's sense of self, and to find hope in the face of overwhelming odds.

In many ways, adapting a story like John's is a tightrope walk between fact and artistic license. The filmmakers had to ensure they were telling John's story with authenticity while also creating a compelling narrative that could stand on its own as a film. The process required extensive research into the actual events that unfolded in John's life, especially the emotional beats of his journey, his struggles with self-worth, his relationships with his family, and the pivotal moments that helped him make sense of the pain he endured.

Joel Courtney, who plays John in the film, went through a thorough preparation process. He worked closely with John O'Leary himself, speaking with him about the nuances of his personality, the challenges he faced, and the impact that the traumatic accident had on his life. For Courtney, it was important to portray not just the physical aspects of John's recovery but the emotional scars that were left behind. The film captures this journey through his portrayal, each small gesture and expression communicates the internal struggle John faced as he learned to embrace his scars and find strength in his vulnerability.

Another challenge was how to present the intense physical transformations John underwent during his recovery. The filmmakers knew they needed to show John's scars realistically, but they also had to navigate the delicate line between showing the rawness of his injuries and maintaining the emotional integrity of the story. The visual representation of his burns and surgeries was meant to be a testament to his strength and survival, but not something that overshadowed his emotional journey. By consulting medical professionals and relying on the advice of John himself, the team created scenes that conveyed the severity of his injuries without sensationalizing them.

The emotional weight of the film was a significant consideration during the writing process. John's life story is deeply personal, and the filmmakers had to respect the emotional territory they were entering. It was essential to portray the difficult moments, John's despair, his anger, and his moments of questioning faith, with honesty. Yet, they also needed to emphasize the powerful moments of hope and inspiration that ultimately defined John's path forward. The filmmakers worked closely with John to ensure that every moment was true to the experience he lived, allowing his story to come to life in a way that would deeply resonate with audiences.

How the Filmmakers Stayed True to John O'Leary's Story

The heart of *Soul on Fire* is John O'Leary's resilience, his ability to face unthinkable tragedy and not only survive but thrive. The filmmakers understood that this story could easily be lost if it veered too far from John's authentic journey. One of the key ways the filmmakers stayed true to the essence of John's story was by involving him in nearly every aspect of the production process. From the early stages of the screenplay to the final cut of the film, John's voice was always present, guiding the filmmakers and ensuring that the story would be told with the care and accuracy it deserved.

John's involvement went beyond just providing feedback on the script. He also worked closely with Joel Courtney, the actor portraying him, to give him a deep understanding of the emotional layers of his life. In their many conversations, John shared intimate details of his recovery, his struggles, and the people who helped him find his way. For Courtney, playing such a deeply personal role was a responsibility he took seriously. He didn't just want to portray John's story; he wanted to honor it. His commitment to getting John's portrayal right, capturing both his vulnerability and strength, was a key factor in the authenticity of the film.

The filmmakers also made sure to capture the real spirit of John's family. The relationship between John and his mother, played by **Stéphanie Szostak**, is particularly important in the film. The filmmakers understood that this bond was a cornerstone of John's recovery and emotional healing. The intimate moments between John and his family were portrayed with sincerity and love, reflecting the true closeness that existed between John and his parents. **Szostak's performance** as John's mother was particularly moving, as it conveyed the deep pain of watching her child suffer and the overwhelming love that kept her going through it all.

The film also respected the role of Jack Buck, portrayed by **William H. Macy**. Jack's mentorship and belief in John were central to his recovery, and the filmmakers made sure to show their relationship with authenticity and respect. In real life, Jack Buck's friendship with John was vital to his healing process, and **Macy's portrayal** of this bond captures the quiet strength that Jack offered. The filmmakers worked to ensure that this relationship was not reduced to a mere plot point but treated with the depth and seriousness it deserved, as it was an essential part of John's emotional journey.

In terms of location, filming in St. Louis was another key element that helped keep the film true to John's story. The filmmakers chose to shoot in the actual locations that played an integral role in John's life. From his family's home to the hospital where he spent months recovering, these locations provided an authentic backdrop for the film, helping the audience connect to the real places where John's healing took place. The filmmakers worked closely with local experts and individuals who had been involved in John's recovery to ensure that the film's portrayal of St. Louis was accurate and respectful to the community that supported John during his darkest days.

Interviews with the Director and Cast on Creating the Movie

The process of bringing *Soul on Fire* to life was one that involved deep collaboration between the director, cast, and crew. Interviews with the director, Sean McNamara, and the cast reveal the challenges, inspirations, and decisions behind the making of the film.

McNamara, in interviews, often spoke about the importance of capturing the emotional truth of John's journey. He described how the film wasn't just about portraying the physical aspects of John's recovery but about showing the internal struggles he faced. For McNamara, the challenge was not only to show John's physical scars but to convey the emotional scars that came with them. He explained how he worked closely with **Courtney** to ensure that John's inner conflict, his shame, his anger, and his eventual acceptance, was portrayed with sensitivity. The relationship between John and Jack Buck was also something McNamara knew had to be treated with care. In interviews, he spoke about how **Macy's portrayal** of Jack was critical to the emotional depth of the film, as it was Jack's belief in John that became the catalyst for much of his healing.

In interviews, **Joel Courtney** reflected on the difficulty of portraying such a deeply personal role. He admitted that he was initially apprehensive about portraying someone whose life was so raw and public. However, after spending time with John and learning about his experiences, Courtney became deeply committed to honoring his journey. In his conversations with John, Courtney learned not just about the events that shaped his life, but also about the resilience that had guided him through it all. Courtney often spoke about the responsibility he felt in portraying John as authentically as possible, and how he wanted to ensure that the portrayal would be something John would be proud of.

Stéphanie Szostak, who played John's mother, spoke emotionally about the role and what it meant to portray such a significant part of John's life. She explained that her portrayal was informed by the deep love and devotion that John's mother felt for her son. Szostak shared how she spent time with John's family and learned about the emotional toll the experience took on them. She described the role as both heartbreaking and inspiring, as it allowed her to connect deeply with the emotional core of the film.

Through these interviews, it's clear that the process of creating *Soul on Fire* was one marked by a commitment to authenticity. The director and cast all approached their roles with the understanding that they were telling a story that was not just John's but one that had the power to inspire and uplift others.

Filming in St. Louis: The Significance of Location

Filming in St. Louis was essential to capturing the true essence of John O'Leary's story. The filmmakers made the decision to shoot on location in the city where John grew up, where he faced the devastation of the fire, and where he ultimately rebuilt his life. This choice was vital, as it helped bring an additional layer of authenticity to the film. The locations themselves, John's home, the hospital where he received treatment, and even the streets of St. Louis, played a significant role in shaping the film's emotional tone.

By filming in the actual places that were pivotal in John's journey, the filmmakers were able to immerse themselves in the environment that shaped the story. The authenticity of these locations provided the cast and crew with a deeper connection to the material. For **Courtney**, filming in John's childhood neighborhood added a layer of meaning to his portrayal. He spoke about how filming in these familiar locations helped him better understand John's emotional connection to the place, and how that sense of home became a part of John's healing process.

Filming in St. Louis also allowed the filmmakers to work with local experts and community members who had been a part of John's recovery. The hospital scenes, in particular, were filmed in a way that reflected the real medical environment John had faced, which helped bring a sense of realism to those moments. The filmmakers consulted with doctors, nurses, and others involved in John's recovery to ensure that the medical procedures and challenges were portrayed accurately.

Chapter 8: The Screenplay – Crafting the Story from Real Events

Adapting John O'Leary's Memoir into a Film Script

Adapting John O'Leary's memoir *On Fire* into a screenplay was a process that required sensitivity, creativity, and a deep understanding of the emotional core of his journey. The transition from the written word to a visual medium is never a straightforward task, but with a story as personal and impactful as John's, the stakes were especially high. The filmmakers had the unique challenge of telling a real-life story that was both raw and deeply emotional, while also ensuring that it would translate effectively to the screen.

John's memoir is filled with personal anecdotes, reflections, and the wisdom he gained from his tragic accident. But as is the case with any memoir, there are elements that simply can't be portrayed in a visual format. The goal of the screenwriters was to capture the heart of John's story, his inner emotional struggles, his family's role in his healing, and the monumental shift in his outlook on life. To do this, they had to find ways to represent the themes of survival, pain, and resilience in a way that would resonate with an audience.

One of the biggest challenges in adapting a memoir into a screenplay is choosing which events to highlight. John's life after the fire was filled with years of recovery, both physical and emotional, which was not only complex but also deeply personal. To ensure that the film didn't get bogged down in an overwhelming amount of detail, the writers had to focus on key events that would push John's character forward and showcase his transformation.

The film opens with the tragedy of the fire, setting the stage for John's story. But in adapting the memoir, the writers had to pick the key moments in John's recovery to create a narrative arc. The process involved distilling the essence of John's emotional and physical healing into a series of scenes that would allow the audience to connect deeply with him as a person, not just a survivor of tragedy. The emotional core of the story, the support of his family, the mentoring relationship with Jack Buck, and John's internal journey of self-acceptance, became the foundation of the screenplay.

One of the most poignant decisions was to focus on the intimate, internal moments of John's recovery. The film could have easily focused solely on the external struggle, his surgeries, his pain, and the challenges he faced in the hospital. But the writers and filmmakers knew that the real power of John's story lay in how he dealt with the emotional aftermath of the accident. How did John reconcile the child he once was with the adult he had become? This question became central to the narrative and was woven into the screenplay's structure.

John O'Leary's own involvement in the adaptation process was invaluable. He worked closely with the screenwriters to ensure that the film stayed true to his experiences, offering insight into the moments that mattered most. In addition to the memoir, the filmmakers conducted numerous interviews with John, giving them a deeper understanding of the emotional and psychological battles he faced. This close collaboration was critical in making sure that John's story would be faithfully represented on screen. His input provided essential guidance on the nuances of his recovery, as well as the small, quiet moments that were pivotal in his transformation.

The screenplay had to juggle multiple layers, telling the story of survival and healing while also exploring John's emotional journey. The act of healing wasn't just physical; it was deeply psychological and spiritual. These aspects of the story were crucial to convey, and the writers used a blend of dialogue, internal monologues, and visual storytelling to bring them to life. The way John learned to accept his scars and ultimately find purpose in his pain became the spine of the screenplay, driving the emotional trajectory of the film.

The casting decisions also played a pivotal role in shaping the way the screenplay came to life. **Joel Courtney**, who plays John, needed to embody not just the physical struggle but the internal evolution of John as well. The depth of Courtney's performance allowed the screenplay to come to life in a way that wasn't simply about recovering from trauma but about transforming that trauma into a life of meaning. John's relationship with **William H. Macy's Jack Buck** also added emotional weight to the film, representing the mentorship and hope that was central to John's healing.

Balancing Accuracy with Cinematic Creativity

While the goal was always to remain true to John's life and the reality of his experience, the filmmakers also had to find ways to make his story engaging and visually compelling. This meant making creative decisions about how to represent certain events, how to condense a long period of time into a two-hour film, and how to convey the emotional depth of John's journey without getting bogged down in unnecessary details.

One key area where creativity played a significant role was in how the film approached John's physical healing. In real life, John underwent countless surgeries and treatments that stretched over years. However, a film adaptation cannot simply show years of recovery in a linear way. Instead, the filmmakers chose to highlight key moments that would visually communicate the most significant aspects of John's healing process. The film didn't linger on every medical detail but instead focused on moments of personal transformation, John's first time seeing himself in the mirror after the surgeries, the internal conflict he felt in accepting his new self, and his eventual journey toward self-empowerment.

The scene in which John looks at himself in the mirror for the first time after the surgeries is a pivotal moment in the film. This scene was not just about showing his physical scars, but about capturing the emotional weight of the moment. It represents John coming to terms with his new identity, and it's a moment that speaks to the broader human experience of accepting oneself, flaws and all. This moment is emotionally intense, and the filmmakers used creative cinematography to enhance the feeling of isolation and self-doubt John experienced. The reflective surface of the mirror was used as a metaphor for John's journey of self-reflection and self-acceptance.

In terms of dialogue, the film had to condense years of inner turmoil and healing into brief exchanges that could communicate the depth of John's emotions. The balance between staying true to the essence of John's memoir and creating an engaging cinematic experience meant that some of the more detailed aspects of John's story had to be streamlined. However, the key moments of emotional growth and realization remained intact. In particular, the conversations between John and **Jack Buck** became critical in driving home the film's core messages of resilience and hope.

One of the most significant creative choices in the adaptation process was how the filmmakers depicted John's relationship with his family. In the film, **Stéphanie Szostak** and **John Corbett**, who play John's mother and father, respectively, bring depth to the family dynamic. The love and support they offer John is a key part of his recovery, and the filmmakers made sure to show this relationship in a way that was both authentic and emotionally powerful. While much of John's recovery is depicted as an individual journey, the film never forgets the importance of family and community in the healing process.

The balance of accuracy and creativity also extended to the portrayal of the hospital scenes. Instead of showing every procedure John underwent, the filmmakers focused on the emotional experience of being in a hospital, dealing with pain, fear, and isolation. Through the use of visual effects and careful pacing, the filmmakers created an experience that felt both real and emotionally charged, allowing the audience to feel the intensity of John's physical suffering without overwhelming them with graphic details.

Key Dialogues and Monologues That Define the Film

The power of the film lies not only in its visual storytelling but in the impactful dialogues and monologues that bring John's emotional journey to life. These moments of dialogue often serve as pivotal turning points in the film, allowing John and the other characters to express their inner thoughts and struggles. Through these key moments, the audience is able to connect with the characters on a deeper level, understanding their motivations and the emotional complexities they face.

One of the most powerful moments in the film occurs when **William H. Macy's Jack Buck** delivers a pivotal line of dialogue to John. As John lies in the hospital, feeling defeated and unsure of his future, Jack looks at him and says, "You can't control what happens to you, but you can control what you do with it." This line encapsulates the central theme of the film, the idea that we can't always control the circumstances we face, but we can control how we respond. Jack's words become a turning point for John, motivating him to take control of his story and use his pain as fuel for growth.

Another key moment of dialogue comes later in the film when John, having come to terms with his scars, speaks to a group of people about his journey. This speech is a culmination of his transformation. The monologue is powerful because it shows how far John has come, not just physically, but emotionally. In this moment, John articulates the lessons he has learned about strength, vulnerability, and the power of hope. The speech encapsulates the heart of John's message: that despite the darkest times, we can always choose to find meaning, to rise above, and to help others along the way.

The film also features a deeply emotional conversation between John and his mother, played by **Stéphanie Szostak**. In this moment, his mother reassures him that he is not defined by his scars. "Your worth isn't measured by what you see in the mirror," she tells him. This dialogue represents the emotional core of John's recovery, as it speaks to the universal struggle of self-acceptance. It is through these simple, heartfelt moments of dialogue that the emotional weight of the film truly hits home.

Chapter 9: Filmmaking Techniques: Visualizing Hope and Struggle

Using Color and Lighting to Portray Emotion

Color and lighting are two of the most powerful tools filmmakers have in their arsenal to communicate emotion, set the tone, and shape the visual storytelling of a film. In *Soul on Fire*, these elements are used not only to create atmosphere but to deepen the emotional impact of John O'Leary's journey. From the warm, golden hues of his childhood to the cold, sterile lighting of the hospital, every scene is carefully lit to evoke specific emotions and underline the themes of the film.

In the early scenes of the film, when John is a carefree boy playing in the garage, the lighting is soft and warm, almost reminiscent of the golden light of a summer afternoon. The colors are rich with warmth, showcasing the innocence and joy of childhood. The filmmakers wanted to emphasize the sense of freedom that John felt before the accident. There is a glow to the scenes that highlights the optimism of his early years, as if his world was filled with light and possibility. This warmth reflects John's pre-accident state, a boy who believed the world was full of hope and wonder.

As the narrative shifts to the traumatic accident and the aftermath of the fire, the color palette and lighting change drastically. The warmth fades, replaced by harsh, cold lighting that captures the sterility of the hospital and the emotional isolation that John begins to feel. The lighting becomes more clinical and shadowy, with shadows creeping across John's face to reflect the internal darkness he is wrestling with. The fire, of course, is depicted as an intense, fiery orange and red, representing the overwhelming chaos and devastation of the moment. The lighting in this section is sharp, and the colors are saturated with the intensity of fear and destruction, emphasizing the unrelenting nature of the disaster that altered John's life forever.

But the film also uses subtle shifts in lighting to reflect John's emotional recovery. As he begins to regain his strength, both physically and emotionally, the lighting gradually brightens. In scenes where John reconnects with his family or begins to open up to Jack Buck, there's a noticeable warmth that returns to the scenes. The light softens around John, and the shadows that once defined him begin to recede. It's a visual representation of his healing process, emotionally, mentally, and spiritually. This shift in lighting is not only a cinematic choice but an emotional one, reminding the audience that healing isn't just about fixing the body; it's about finding light in the darkest moments.

The use of color in the film is also significant in depicting the contrast between John's physical and emotional states. When John is isolated in the hospital, surrounded by the stark, cold lights of the medical world, the colors are muted and washed out, reinforcing his feeling of being trapped in a world he can't control. Yet, as he begins to reclaim his life, the colors in the scenes gradually become more vibrant, symbolizing his renewed sense of purpose and his ability to see hope, even in the most challenging times. This visual progression mirrors the psychological journey John undergoes, making the audience feel his growth through the visual landscape of the film.

These shifts in lighting and color don't just serve as technical aspects of filmmaking; they are deeply embedded in the emotional arcs of the characters. The visual choices reflect not just John's external environment but his internal transformation. The filmmakers were able to use these elements to emphasize the most profound moments of John's journey, helping to create a visual language that resonates with the audience on a deeper emotional level.

Special Effects and Realism in the Depiction of the Fire

The depiction of the fire in *Soul on Fire* is undoubtedly one of the most crucial and challenging aspects of the film. Not only does the fire serve as the inciting incident that sets the entire story into motion, but it also represents the emotional and physical destruction that John faces. The special effects used to bring the fire to life had to balance realism with artistic storytelling. The filmmakers needed to portray the fire in a way that was both visually striking and true to the gravity of the real-life event without sensationalizing it or making it feel too over-the-top.

In the early scenes, when the fire erupts in the garage, the special effects team used a combination of practical and digital effects to create a fiery explosion that is as harrowing as it is visually intense. The filmmakers chose to depict the fire in a way that reflected its chaotic, unpredictable nature. The flames that engulf John are shown in an almost exaggerated manner, as if they are an unstoppable force of nature. The smoke, the heat, and the intensity of the fire are portrayed in such a way that the audience can almost feel the oppressive atmosphere. The explosion itself is brief but devastating, and the use of sound and visual effects makes the moment feel both immediate and terrifying.

The decision to use digital effects to show the fire was crucial in ensuring that the sequence felt realistic and impactful. However, the filmmakers also knew that they had to balance the intensity of the fire with a more intimate portrayal of John's experience. The focus wasn't just on the destruction of the garage; it was on John's immediate reaction to the flames, his terror, and the pain he endured as the fire consumed him. The realism of the fire is grounded in the human experience of trauma, making the scene feel even more visceral and immediate.

What's truly remarkable about the fire scenes is how they're not just visually arresting, but they're deeply symbolic. The flames represent more than just the physical destruction of the garage, they represent the loss of innocence, the brutal nature of the accident, and the emotional scars that John will carry for the rest of his life. The filmmakers understood that the fire needed to be more than just an explosive sequence, it had to serve as a metaphor for the internal chaos that John would struggle with long after the flames had subsided.

Later in the film, the special effects team uses subtle visual effects to show the aftereffects of the fire on John's body. The scars that mark John's face and arms are depicted in a way that feels raw and unflinching. The team worked closely with makeup artists to create realistic burns and scars that would reflect the physical toll of the fire. This decision to showcase the scars in such a detailed and realistic way was important, as it underscored the emotional weight of the recovery process. The audience is not shielded from the full reality of John's injuries, he is shown as he truly was, a young boy who survived against all odds, his body forever marked by the flames. This raw depiction of his scars becomes a key part of his transformation, showing that these marks, which initially symbolized his pain, would ultimately come to represent his strength.

The Power of Flashbacks: Telling John's Story Within a Story

One of the most effective storytelling techniques in *Soul on Fire* is the use of flashbacks. Flashbacks serve as a way to tell John's story within the larger narrative, providing the audience with glimpses into his life before and after the fire. These scenes help deepen the emotional resonance of the film, allowing the audience to experience John's transformation not just through his present-day recovery, but through moments from his past that shaped who he became.

The flashbacks are strategically placed throughout the film to create contrast between John's life before the accident and the person he becomes afterward. In the opening scenes, we see John as a carefree child, full of energy and joy. These moments are peaceful and light, filmed with warm tones and gentle lighting, reflecting the innocence of his early years. As the film progresses, these flashbacks become more poignant. The once joyful moments are now tinged with a sense of loss, as John must grapple with the stark reality of the person he has become.

The flashbacks are not just simple recollections of past events; they serve as emotional markers in John's recovery process. The filmmakers use flashbacks to show how John's trauma didn't just happen in the hospital, it was something that reverberated throughout his entire life. Through these glimpses into his past, we see the emotional scars that were left behind, as well as the moments of strength and resilience that allowed him to move forward.

The relationship between John and his family is also explored through flashbacks. In one particularly emotional flashback, we see John's mother comforting him in the hospital after his first surgery. The tender, quiet moments between them offer insight into the unwavering love and support that would play such a crucial role in John's emotional healing. These flashbacks are a powerful reminder that recovery doesn't happen in isolation, it is deeply connected to the people who love and support us.

Perhaps one of the most impactful uses of flashbacks comes when John reflects on his relationship with Jack Buck. The film transitions from the present-day John, now a young man and motivational speaker, back to the moments when Jack was a constant presence in his life. The flashbacks of Jack's visits to the hospital provide a deeper understanding of how Jack's mentorship shaped John's healing process. In these moments, the audience witnesses John's internal transformation from a young boy full of self-doubt to a man who begins to embrace his scars and see them as symbols of strength rather than signs of weakness.

The filmmakers use these flashbacks to illustrate the progression of John's emotional recovery, showing that the road to healing is often nonlinear. It's not just about the physical recovery that took place in the hospital; it's about the emotional journey that followed, one marked by self-reflection, moments of despair, and, eventually, the realization that he could use his past to inspire others.

Chapter 10: Overcoming Adversity – Lessons from John's Journey

The Importance of Resilience in the Face of Tragedy

John O'Leary's journey is a testament to the profound power of resilience. Resilience is often described as the ability to bounce back from adversity, but John's story goes beyond merely surviving hardship, his journey reveals the true depth of what resilience means. Resilience is not just about enduring pain; it's about facing suffering, grappling with it, and choosing to rise above it, stronger than before. The resilience that John exhibited in the aftermath of the fire is not only what helped him survive but is at the core of the movie's larger message: that adversity can be overcome, no matter how insurmountable it might seem.

The film *Soul on Fire* highlights John's resilience from the moment of the fire itself. The way the filmmakers chose to present the immediate aftermath of the accident, showing John's physical suffering in stark detail, sets the stage for his emotional resilience. After the fire, when John was given little chance of survival, the doctors were unsure whether he would ever recover fully, either physically or emotionally. However, John's resilience wasn't just about enduring pain; it was about his refusal to be defined by his trauma.

Joel Courtney's portrayal of John captures this resilience in a way that is profoundly moving. His performance doesn't merely depict a boy who is tough and able to survive, but one who chooses to transform his pain into something empowering. Early in his recovery, John doesn't have all the answers. He's confused, angry, and, at times, he loses hope. The film does not shy away from showing these moments of struggle. What it does so effectively, however, is to depict how resilience is often not a singular moment but a gradual evolution. Resilience is not a trait you're born with; it is something you cultivate over time. John's resilience grew through his daily battles, through his interactions with his family, and through the relationships that he built with others, like Jack Buck.

As the story progresses, John learns that resilience isn't just about surviving physical pain; it's about how you rise up mentally and emotionally. He begins to accept his scars, not as marks of shame, but as symbols of his strength. His journey is one of transforming adversity into opportunity. Through his journey, viewers come to understand that resilience isn't a trait limited to a few, it's something we all have the capacity for, if we choose to cultivate it in our lives. John's story is a reminder that, no matter how dark life may seem, there is always a path forward, and that path is often forged through resilience.

The resilience of John's character is mirrored in the resilience of those around him. His family, his mother, father, and siblings, are also symbols of resilience. The pain of watching John suffer, and their unwavering support, shows that resilience can often be collective. John's story of survival and recovery wouldn't have been possible without the love and belief of those closest to him, especially his mother, played by **Stéphanie Szostak**, who consistently reminds him that his scars do not define him. Their collective strength becomes a defining theme throughout the film, and it underscores that resilience is not just about individual strength, but about the strength we find through our relationships with others.

How the Movie Inspires Viewers to Never Give Up

One of the central themes of *Soul on Fire* is its ability to inspire viewers to never give up, no matter the challenges they face. The film does not offer a false sense of hope; it doesn't suggest that everything will be okay all the time. Instead, it presents a more nuanced and honest depiction of the human spirit, showing that even in our darkest hours, we have the ability to push forward and find hope.

For John, the path to never giving up wasn't always clear. In fact, there were many moments in his journey where he doubted whether it was worth continuing, especially in the wake of such devastating physical and emotional pain. There are scenes in the film where **Joel Courtney's portrayal** of John is so raw and vulnerable that it's impossible not to feel the weight of his struggles. These moments are not only relatable for viewers who have gone through their own hardships but are a testament to the authenticity of the film's storytelling. The movie does not shy away from showing the painful reality of trauma, it doesn't promise that the journey will be easy. Instead, it offers a realistic portrayal of what it means to face overwhelming adversity and find a way to push through.

One of the film's key scenes that inspires this message of never giving up comes when John is in the hospital, struggling to find any reason to keep going. His body is broken, and his spirit feels as if it might break along with it. Yet, it is in this moment of extreme vulnerability that John begins to understand something vital: survival isn't just about physical recovery. It's about finding meaning, purpose, and strength through the pain. The turning point in John's emotional journey happens when he starts seeing his suffering not as something that defines him, but as something that can fuel his growth. This realization is an important moment in the film, as it's the moment John starts to embrace his future and his story.

The filmmakers use these pivotal moments to encourage the viewer to look inward and find strength when things seem impossible. They show how important it is to persevere, even when the future feels uncertain. Through John's journey, we learn that giving up isn't an option, it's about how we respond to adversity. The story of John O'Leary proves that, even in the face of tragedy, there is always a way forward, and sometimes, that path forward is paved by never giving up.

The influence of **William H. Macy's Jack Buck** plays a significant role in John's own realization of this. Jack's unwavering belief in John, even when John couldn't believe in himself, teaches us the power of having someone who supports us in the hardest of times. Jack's character isn't just a mentor in a traditional sense; he's a beacon of hope, someone who shows John that even in the depths of suffering, there is always a light to follow. Macy's portrayal of Jack is understated but powerful, he gives John the courage to fight on when he feels like giving up.

Finding Strength in Vulnerability: Embracing Pain to Heal

One of the most profound messages of *Soul on Fire* is the idea that true strength comes from embracing vulnerability. For John O'Leary, vulnerability was initially something he struggled with. After the fire, he wanted to hide his scars, both physically and emotionally. He didn't want to be seen as weak or broken. However, as his healing journey unfolded, John realized that true healing didn't come from hiding his pain, it came from embracing it, understanding it, and sharing it with others.

In the film, there are several moments where John's vulnerability is on full display. One of the most powerful scenes occurs when he stands in front of a mirror and looks at the scars that mark his body. This is a deeply vulnerable moment, not just physically, but emotionally. It's in this moment that John has to confront who he has become and who he is still trying to be. He could have easily turned away from the mirror, as many people in his situation might have done. Instead, he looks at his reflection, understanding that his scars are a part of him, and they do not diminish his worth.

Joel Courtney's performance in this scene is exceptionally moving. There's no dialogue in this moment, but the emotions are clear through his facial expressions and body language. The film doesn't shy away from the rawness of this moment, John is vulnerable, and it's in this vulnerability that he begins to find his true strength. The filmmakers use this silence to show how John's true healing process begins when he stops hiding from his pain and instead allows himself to be vulnerable and open to the world.

The message is clear: strength isn't about being invincible or hiding from pain. It's about embracing that pain, acknowledging it, and learning from it. By embracing his scars, both physical and emotional, John is able to reclaim his life. His vulnerability doesn't make him weak; it makes him stronger. This is an essential lesson for anyone facing adversity, and the film does an incredible job of illustrating this concept through John's journey.

The theme of finding strength in vulnerability is reinforced throughout the movie, especially through John's relationship with his family. His mother's unconditional love and belief in him, as portrayed by **Stéphanie Szostak**, is a powerful reminder that healing happens when we allow ourselves to be supported by others. She shows John that being open about his pain doesn't make him lesser, it makes him human. The support from his family gives him the courage to embrace his vulnerability and, in doing so, find the strength to move forward.

In *Soul on Fire*, John O'Leary's journey is not just one of survival, but of profound transformation. The film offers viewers a powerful reminder that overcoming adversity is about more than just enduring, it's about finding strength through vulnerability, embracing pain as a part of healing, and never giving up, no matter the odds. John's resilience in the face of tragedy is a testament to the power of the human spirit, and his story continues to inspire others to push through their own struggles.

Through **Joel Courtney's portrayal** of John, **William H. Macy's mentorship** as Jack Buck, and the heartfelt performances of the supporting cast, the film captures the essence of John's message: that no matter how dark the path may seem, there is always a way forward, and it is through our vulnerability and pain that we find our true strength.

Chapter 11: Faith and Hope – Core Themes in *Soul on Fire*

The Role of Faith in John O'Leary's Recovery

Faith is not only a central element of John O'Leary's personal journey but also an essential theme throughout *Soul on Fire*. The film portrays faith not just as a religious concept but as a deeply personal and transformative force. In the wake of the tragic fire that changed his life, John's faith played an undeniable role in his healing process, physically, emotionally, and spiritually. The way the filmmakers choose to depict faith in the movie goes beyond simple religious rituals; it explores faith as a mindset, a belief system, and a vital lifeline in moments of overwhelming adversity.

For John, faith was initially about survival. After the fire, when John was in the hospital fighting for his life, his faith was tested in the most intense way possible. The early scenes in the film highlight John's deep uncertainty about his future. At times, he questions whether he will even make it through the night, let alone ever live a meaningful life again. During these moments, faith emerges not just as a comforting thought but as a quiet force that drives him to push forward, despite all the odds.

Stéphanie Szostak's portrayal of John's mother is integral in showing how faith sustained the family, especially in the darkest moments. Her belief that John could heal, both physically and spiritually, never wavered. As she stays by his side, praying for his recovery, it's clear that her faith isn't simply in the idea that God will heal him; it's in her belief that John has the strength within himself to fight and recover. This distinction is important, the film portrays faith not as a magical solution but as an active, participatory process in John's recovery.

The spiritual aspect of John's recovery is subtly depicted through his moments of reflection and quiet prayer. **Joel Courtney**, playing John, captures these internal moments of faith with subtlety and depth. In one particularly moving scene, John, still recovering in the hospital, quietly prays as he contemplates his future. This moment is not loud or dramatic but is instead deeply personal and introspective. Through this scene, the filmmakers convey that faith is not just about belief in a higher power, but about finding the strength to endure and accept one's circumstances.

John's faith is also reflected in his relationship with **William H. Macy's Jack Buck.** Jack serves as a mentor, but his influence on John's faith is more subtle. While Jack's guidance is rooted in practical wisdom and encouragement, it is also shaped by his own belief in the power of resilience and the human spirit. Their conversations often revolve around the idea of believing in oneself even when the world seems dark. This is where faith, as depicted in the film, is deeply intertwined with hope. It's a belief that even in the hardest times, there is a reason to keep going.

Through Jack's mentorship and the support of his family, John begins to rebuild his faith, not just in God, but in himself. This transformative process is not just about recovering from the burns, but about reclaiming his life. By the end of the film, John's faith becomes less about questioning his survival and more about embracing the strength he has gained from the struggle. He begins to see that his faith was never about waiting for a miracle but about trusting that he could create meaning from his pain.

The film beautifully weaves John's journey of faith with his growth as a person. In the final scenes, when John speaks about his recovery, there's a quiet assurance in his voice. He has come to understand that faith, for him, is about accepting the past and finding purpose in it. Faith has become a source of empowerment, a way for John to not only survive but thrive. The filmmakers use this evolution of John's faith to communicate a powerful message: faith, in all its forms, is essential to overcoming adversity.

Hope as a Central Theme: The Motivation Behind the Film

Hope is the driving force behind *Soul on Fire*. From the very first moments of the film, when John's life is shattered by the explosion in the garage, to the final, triumphant scenes where he finds peace with his scars and begins a new chapter as a motivational speaker, hope is a constant theme that propels the story forward. It's not just about finding hope after tragedy; it's about how hope can fuel the entire recovery process, enabling individuals to confront their darkest moments and come out stronger.

In the early part of the film, hope comes in small doses. After John is severely burned, he struggles with the idea of ever being "normal" again. The film doesn't present an easy path of recovery, John's journey is long, filled with pain, self-doubt, and setbacks. Yet, in these moments of despair, we see the first glimpses of hope: in the loving faces of his family, in the steadfast belief of Jack Buck, and in John's own quiet resolve to keep going. These early seeds of hope are critical because they show how, even in the darkest moments, hope is something that must be cultivated, nurtured by small acts of faith, resilience, and connection.

As John's journey progresses, hope becomes a larger theme. Hope isn't just a feeling of optimism; it is an active force that drives John forward. **William H. Macy's Jack Buck** embodies this idea of hope. Jack is the character who continually reminds John that life isn't over, even when it feels like the world has collapsed. Jack's belief in John, his consistent encouragement and his refusal to let John give up, is the catalyst for John's emotional growth. Jack's mentorship is a powerful reminder that hope is often most potent when it is shared with others. The movie depicts how, when someone believes in you, even when you can't believe in yourself, it provides the spark of hope that can lead to transformation.

The filmmakers used John's emotional evolution to demonstrate that hope is not just about waiting for things to get better, it's about finding meaning and strength in the face of adversity. As John grows stronger, both physically and emotionally, his hope begins to shift from simply surviving to living with purpose. The transition from despair to hope is portrayed with authenticity, reflecting the slow but steady process of finding light in a world that can sometimes feel overwhelmingly dark.

John's message of hope extends beyond the film. His story is not just about overcoming a personal tragedy, it's about inspiring others to face their own challenges. The movie captures this universal message with incredible clarity: no matter how insurmountable the struggle, there is always hope, and there is always a way forward. The film is built on the idea that hope isn't just about expecting something good to happen, but about actively choosing to find meaning, purpose, and strength, even when life seems to offer none.

Through **Joel Courtney's performance**, we see John's emotional evolution from someone who is completely consumed by the weight of his scars to someone who begins to find strength and purpose in them. Courtney's portrayal of John is grounded in a quiet optimism, he doesn't have all the answers, but he knows that hope is what will keep him going. It is this hope, more than anything, that becomes the foundation of his recovery.

Spirituality and its Representation in the Movie

Spirituality plays a subtle but important role in *Soul on Fire*. The film doesn't overtly focus on any one religious tradition, but it weaves spirituality into the fabric of John's journey. Spirituality, in this context, is about finding a sense of peace and connection to something greater than oneself. For John, this wasn't necessarily a religious awakening but a spiritual one, a realization that his survival and healing were part of a larger purpose.

The spiritual aspect of the film is most clearly represented through John's relationship with faith and hope. It is not about religious doctrine; rather, it's about the universal idea that there is something more to life than pain and suffering. This realization is a deeply spiritual one for John. The film doesn't try to define spirituality for the audience; instead, it leaves room for personal interpretation, allowing each viewer to find their own connection to the idea of spirituality.

In the hospital scenes, we see John struggling with the idea of his own worth. This struggle isn't just physical; it's spiritual. John questions whether he has any value left after the fire. It is through his moments of reflection and prayer that he begins to reconnect with the deeper aspects of his life. His spirituality is grounded not in religious practices but in the quiet moments where he connects with his inner self and finds peace in the midst of chaos.

The spiritual journey in the film is also represented by the love and support of John's family. **Stéphanie Szostak's portrayal** of his mother, in particular, emphasizes this idea. Her faith and unwavering support for John are spiritually empowering, providing him with the strength he needs to heal. The love she offers him is not just maternal, it is a spiritual force that helps John find the strength to keep moving forward.

In the later stages of the film, as John begins to reclaim his life and find purpose, his spirituality becomes more about sharing his story with others. Through his speeches and his journey as a motivational speaker, John learns that his healing isn't just for himself, it is part of something greater, something that can inspire others to heal as well. This realization is deeply spiritual, as it shows John that his survival was not just a personal victory but a gift he can share with the world.

In *Soul on Fire*, the themes of faith, hope, and spirituality are not just background elements, they are at the heart of John O'Leary's journey. The film beautifully portrays how these forces come together to support John's healing, driving him to overcome adversity and find meaning in his pain. Through **Joel Courtney's performance** as John, **William H. Macy's mentorship** as Jack Buck, and the unwavering love of his family, the movie captures the essence of these core themes, showing that, in the face of tragedy, it is faith, hope, and a connection to something greater that give us the strength to keep going.

As viewers watch John's transformation from a boy who was engulfed in flames to a man who inspires others, they are reminded of the power of these themes in their own lives. The film encourages us to embrace faith, to hold on to hope, and to find spirituality in the journey of healing. Ultimately, *Soul on Fire* is not just a story about overcoming adversity, it is a story about finding strength in the deepest parts of ourselves and using that strength to inspire the world around us.

Chapter 12: Conclusion – A Story of Hope, Strength, and Unbreakable Spirit

Wrapping Up the Story Behind *Soul on Fire*

Soul on Fire is not just a film; it is a journey into the heart of resilience, the power of transformation, and the indomitable human spirit. From its gripping opening moments to its final, uplifting conclusion, the film takes viewers through an emotional rollercoaster that mirrors John O'Leary's own path to recovery after a tragic accident that left him with severe burns. What makes *Soul on Fire* stand out is its ability to take a personal, almost unfathomable story of survival and turn it into a universal narrative about strength, faith, and the capacity to overcome life's greatest challenges.

At its core, *Soul on Fire* is a testament to the unyielding power of the human spirit. It explores John's journey not just as a survivor but as someone who transforms his deepest suffering into an inspiration for others. While the film is centered on John's life, it resonates with anyone who has faced their own personal struggles, whether they are physical, emotional, or spiritual. Through John's eyes, we see that no matter how overwhelming life's obstacles may seem, there is always a path to healing, growth, and strength.

Through **Joel Courtney's** powerful portrayal of John, the film brings to life the emotional complexity of this real-life hero's story. Courtney doesn't just portray a boy who survived a tragedy; he embodies the journey of healing, one that is not linear but full of setbacks, moments of despair, and the quiet strength that emerges from within. John's evolution from a broken boy to a man who inspires millions is captured with authenticity and raw emotion, making the film a deeply moving experience.

But the film isn't just about the story of one man. It's about how we, as individuals, can rise above our own struggles. It's about how, even when the road ahead seems impossible, there is always hope, always strength, and always the possibility for transformation. John's journey shows that we don't have to walk this path alone, whether through faith, family, or mentorship, the support of others is crucial in overcoming adversity.

The central themes of faith, hope, and resilience that run throughout *Soul on Fire* create a tapestry of human connection and personal empowerment. The film's conclusion doesn't just close the story of John's life, it opens the door for viewers to see their own struggles through a lens of possibility, reminding them that no matter the depth of their pain, they, too, have the strength to rise above it.

Final Thoughts on the Impact of John O'Leary's Journey

John O'Leary's journey, as depicted in *Soul on Fire*, is more than a remarkable tale of survival, it is an ongoing movement. After the fire, when John was given little chance of survival, no one could have imagined that he would not only recover physically but would go on to inspire millions with his story. His journey wasn't just about learning to live again; it was about learning to live with purpose. The strength that John showed, first in his recovery and later in his work as a motivational speaker, is what gives his story its universal appeal.

What truly sets John's journey apart from others is not the scale of the tragedy he faced, but his transformation after it. The film captures how John shifted from a place of self-pity and despair into a place of hope and service, finding meaning in the very scars that once filled him with shame. His story shows that even in the aftermath of life's most painful experiences, we can choose to find purpose, and through that purpose, inspire others.

In addition to his physical recovery, John's emotional and spiritual recovery is the core of his journey. The pain he endured, both physical and emotional, was immense, but the journey through it, the decision to embrace his scars, is what makes his story so powerful. It's the realization that his scars didn't make him weaker but instead became a symbol of his strength and resilience.

John's role as a motivational speaker, where he shares his story with the world, further exemplifies his deep understanding of what it means to overcome. His ability to take what could have been a story of defeat and turn it into one of empowerment and inspiration is what makes his journey resonate across generations. Whether he's speaking to a group of young students, cancer patients, or corporate leaders, John's message is always the same: no matter the circumstances, we are not defined by our pain or our past. We are defined by how we rise from it.

Through his work, John continues to inspire others to see their own potential for transformation, proving that, even when we are faced with seemingly insurmountable challenges, we have the power to shape our own destinies. The film brings this reality to life, offering audiences a poignant reminder that hope is not a passive wish but an active force that, when embraced, can lead to incredible change.

What Audiences Can Take Away from the Film

Soul on Fire is a film that doesn't just ask audiences to watch a story unfold, it challenges them to engage with it on a deeply personal level. John O'Leary's story is universal in its themes of overcoming adversity, embracing vulnerability, and finding hope in the darkest of times. While the film is undoubtedly a tribute to John's incredible strength, it is also a powerful call to action for viewers to reflect on their own lives and the way they approach challenges.

There are several key takeaways from the film that have the power to resonate with anyone who has ever faced struggle, suffering, or self-doubt:

1. **Resilience in the Face of Adversity**: One of the most powerful lessons of *Soul on Fire* is the idea that resilience is not just about bouncing back from tragedy, but about embracing the experience, learning from it, and allowing it to shape us. John's recovery wasn't just about physical healing; it was about choosing to find meaning in his suffering and using it as a foundation for personal growth.

2. **The Power of Faith and Hope**: John's journey illustrates that faith and hope are not simply passive feelings we have in times of crisis; they are active forces that shape how we deal with life's most difficult moments. Whether it's through his belief in himself, his relationship with his family, or his connection to a higher power, John's story reinforces that having faith in something greater than ourselves can provide the

strength to face the impossible.

3. **The Strength Found in Vulnerability**: One of the most profound aspects of John's recovery is his decision to embrace his scars, not just the physical ones but the emotional ones as well. The film shows that vulnerability is not a weakness but a source of strength. By accepting our pain and sharing it with others, we allow ourselves to heal and, in doing so, inspire others to do the same.

4. **The Importance of Community and Support**: John's journey wasn't a solo endeavor. His family, particularly his mother, and his mentor Jack Buck played a pivotal role in his emotional healing. The film emphasizes that while we may face struggles on our own, the support of others is crucial in helping us find our way. Whether through family, friends, or mentors, it's the collective strength of those around us that helps us move forward.

5. **The Power of Storytelling**: John's choice to share his story with the world, despite the pain it involves, is a powerful reminder of the transformative nature of storytelling. By opening up about our struggles, we give others permission

to do the same. John's work as a motivational speaker shows that sharing our pain not only helps us heal but helps others feel less alone in their own battles. His story is an example of how one person's journey can change the lives of many.

In the final scenes of the film, John's story is portrayed as a beacon of hope. His ability to inspire others, to help them see their own potential for strength and transformation, is the ultimate takeaway for audiences. No matter how difficult life may seem, John's journey shows that we all have the capacity to rise above our circumstances and find meaning in our suffering.

Conclusion: A Story of Transformation

Soul on Fire is a deeply moving story of survival, but more importantly, it is a story of transformation. John O'Leary's journey teaches us that, even in the most devastating of circumstances, we have the power to change our lives, to find hope in the darkest times, and to embrace our vulnerabilities as sources of strength. Through **Joel Courtney's powerful performance** as John, **Stéphanie Szostak's portrayal** of his mother, and **William H. Macy's mentorship** as Jack Buck, the film brings John's journey to life in a way that inspires and empowers viewers.

John's story is a living testament to the human capacity to overcome, to endure, and to thrive. It reminds us that hope is not something that is given to us; it is something that we must choose to create in our own lives, every day. *Soul on Fire* leaves audiences with a profound message: that no matter the adversity, the road to healing and transformation is always open, if we have the courage to walk it.

Made in the USA
Monee, IL
30 September 2025